Social Media:

How to Build a Targeted Community
Around a Brand on Social Media

by Ben Gothard,
Founder & CEO of Gothard Enterprises LLC
Author of CEO at 20: A Little Book for Big Dreams

Introduction

Social Media, defined as "any use of digital media, including text, video, images, etc., for communication," is a recent, global phenomenon. With roughly over 2 billion people using some sort of platform, Social Media has become a staple of our society. We are now truly global citizens, connected with the world instantly and more readily than ever before. For businesses, this means that there is a ton of information on and an endless number of ways to reach a specific target audience or market. As with any industry, there are more and less prominent Social Media platforms, each with their own niche. The biggest of these is Facebook with about 1.6 billion monthly active users. People of all ages log onto Facebook to connect with others, share their ideas, and upload text, pictures, and videos in a online, public space. Tumblr, a visual microblogging site with about 555 million monthly active users, is a fierce contender for younger people with about 50% of their users between the ages of 18-34. With about 50% of their 400 million monthly active users between the ages of 18-34, Instagram, owned by Facebook, is a mobile-based platform where people can only upload pictures and videos. Twitter, a microblogging platform, closely follows with about 320 million monthly active users. While Twitter allows pictures and videos, it is a predominantly text-based platform analogous to a news ticker (like on Sports Center or the news). A rising star amongst Social Media platforms is Snapchat. While it sits at around 200 million users a month, it claims about 10 billion daily video views (Smith 2016), a number that surpasses Facebook. The incredible part of this statistic is that every single view is opt-in, meaning people have to click to view! The final platform is LinkedIn, a platform for professional networking, job-hunting, and a place to put your resume online. While LinkedIn only has about 100 million monthly active users, its dominance over the professional side of Social Media will cement its relevance for years to come. With all of these different platforms and audiences, it is incredibly difficult to have a single, all-encompassing marketing plan. However, I want to dive into the fundamentals of one particularly effective marketing strategy: creating a Social Media hub around a brand.

Having started my first company back in December of 2014, I've been wrapping my brain around this idea for two years now. I can confidently say that this marketing strategy is extremely effective, as I help implement it into my clients' businesses every single day. Without fail, the more targeted of a community that I build for my clients, the more successful this strategy is. When people organically seek out your brand for social connection around a central purpose, and your community can provide them with value beyond what they expected, they will come back again and again. A lot of people think that Social Media is fickle, and without purpose and meaningful community as the foundation of your brand's Social Media hubs it is. However, if you can do what 99% of brands fail to do – if you can unite your prospective customers under a single cause or interest – then you'll find that your experience in Social Media will be rich and rewarding. Let's dive into exactly how to do this!

Building a targeted community on Social Media is a three-step process: identifying the ideal community, growing the community through targeting and brand positioning, and managing the community by creating valuable content and developing relationships with the people of the community. The purpose of this book is to analyze these fundamental steps.

The Ideal Community

The first step in building a targeted community on Social Media is to figure out who the ideal community is. In order to discover whom the ideal community is, the term "community" must first be defined. According to Dr. Scott Peck, "the seeds of community reside in humanity." Phil Brown, researcher at Brown University, found five core elements of community, locus (a sense of place), sharing (common interests and perspectives), joint action (a sense of coherence and identity), social ties (creating meaningful relationships), and diversity (multiplicity of sub-communities within the greater whole). I think that these definitions can be sewn together for a profoundly accurate definition of community: a diverse group of people who are gathered together as one around a common interest or problem.

For a brand this provides two main community focal points. On one hand, the interest of the community could be the actual product or service offered. For example, wooden watch enthusiasts would be interested in, and therefore gathered around, wooden watches. For the wooden watch company, the interest in the product itself could drive the community around the brand. For another example, groups of technology enthusiasts take interest in the inner workings of iPhone screens, and would be intrigued by an iPhone screen repair company. The iPhone screen repair company could build the community around their service, gathering those who are naturally interested. On the other hand, a community can come together to solve a particular problem or set of problems. For example, wooden watch enthusiasts might come together to solve the issue of limited lifespans on wooden watches. A wooden watch company could unite these folks around their brand and help this newly formed community solve that problem. The iPhone screen repair company could choose to have their brand champion the fight against screen cracking. That way, people who want to solve the problem of consistent screen cracking (arguably everyone) have a community to be a part of.

To be sure, communities can be based around anything. As long as enough people are willing to stand behind a cause, there can be community, regardless of what that cause is. Take a look at this petition, which, as of December 2016 almost has 50 signatures!

Petition for a Sarcasm font on Social Media Sites

| The Petition | 1 Highlight | 18 Comments | 48 Signatures |

Have you ever tried to make a joke in an internet conversation and the recipient stop talking to you for a week thereafter? Be one of the causes for what could be a revolution in instant messaging for everyone on the planet.

The beauty of community is that there really are no rules, and anyone can stand for anything if they are passionate enough about it. But I digress.

Once the purpose of the community is defined, the population who are going to comprise the community can be accurately identified. More specifically, a brand can understand what makes its ideal customer tick. By labeling the characteristics of a single perfect community member, a brand is able to cater to and attract people who share those qualities in an effort to build the community as a whole. While there are an infinite number of factors to identify a population, I want to focus on two major areas that are particularly useful to building communities around brands: demographics and psychographics.

The most basic demographics and psychographics that every brand should focus on include age, location, gender, income level, education level, marital status, and occupation as well as personality, attitudes, values, interests, hobbies, lifestyles, and behavior, respectively. By knowing this information about your perfect customer, a brand can take create major advantages in the market. For example, a luxury interior design brand's ideal customer could be somebody over 30, married, with a stable job paying over $100,000 a year near the company's store who has a desire to live in a luxurious home regardless of the cost. It would not make sense to target people without the means to buy their items, those who live across the country, or those who value living a simple life. On Social Media, marketers have distinct advantages in that you can target people who meet EXACT criteria using native advertising on all of the platforms. If you know who your buyers are, you can reach them. The trick is figuring out who those buyers are, which is where a fundamental understanding of demographics and psychographics comes in handy.

By identifying the most likely demographic and psychographic of the ideal customer, a brand is able to create marketing advantages, namely three that I want to analyze, in an effort to build a targeted community on Social Media.

The first is lower marketing costs. Marketing can be extremely costly, and according to the Upfront Analytics Team, "medium is one of the factors that essentially decides your budget." The more informed a brand is on its customers, the more efficiently it can allocate its resources to be where those customers are. For example, Pinterest, "a social network that allows users to visually share, and discover new interests by posting images or videos to their own or others' boards and browsing what other users have pinned" (Meng 2014), has a user base comprised of 85% women. A women's clothing brand would be overlooking a powerful medium by not sharing products on Pinterest. Because the platform is visually driven by a demographic that is very likely to be engaged by women's clothing, marketing dollars would go far. On the other hand, the same women's clothing brand might not make the decision to allocate advertising resources to SoundCloud, "an audio platform that lets you listen to what you love and share the sounds you create." While there might be a connection between certain types of music and a woman-centered demographic, it is clear that the dollars spent trying to find customers here would be far less effective for the clothing brand. Instead of relying on a wide net marketing strategy (very far reaching, but not very efficient), demographic and psychographic insights give a brand the information needed to lower marketing costs by targeting only prospective customers.

The second is the ability to identify new opportunities. When analyzing the ideal demographic and psychographic of a specific consumer base, a completely new market segment could be discovered in the process. To take the women's clothing brand example a step further, suppose previous marketing efforts had been reaching women ages 30-65. After diving into the research, the brand might want to adjust their endeavors to include women in the 20-something age range. With over 20 million women in that age range in the United States alone according the 2010 Census, the brand is positioning itself to reach significantly more potential costumers! While new opportunities discovered might not be as immense as the women's clothing brand example, there is huge potential in untapped market segments for brands to explore. In addition to reaching new customers, demographic and psychographic insights could point your brand to a much needed addition or innovation to your existing products. Continuing with the women's clothing brand example, market research could uncover that in this brand's community exists an unsatisfied need for scarves. Not only could the brand reach its existing community in fresh ways with the new scarves, but the community would also grow in size as it takes a slice of market share from the scarf industry. However, without the demographic and psychographic analysis, the women's clothing brand would not have been able to cater to its community.

The third marketing advantage is creating unique selling points. Demographic and psychographic research can help a brand "create and define scenarios to which [its] customers can relate" (Upfront Analytics Team). For example, refrigerated dip brands are likely to find customers who relate to those products during the Super Bowl because a significant amount of Super Bowl viewers are at parties where refrigerated dip is served. According to a study of the 2015 Super Bowl by Statista, "refrigerated dips saw the largest increase in dollar sales with 47.76 percent during the week leading up to the Super Bowl." Instead of just trying to toss the product into the market, refrigerated dip brands can tap into the extremely relatable Super Bowl party scenario. Instead of being sold on an ordinary item, the customer is part of the action – a very powerful buying impetus. By understanding demographic and psychographic insights, brands can create an experience for its ideal customer, a truly distinct selling point.

I get really excited whenever I get to teach market targeting because what my company, Gothard Enterprises, does best is leverage paid advertising to send highly targeted traffic to a specific website, landing page, product page, etc. By testing out different demographic and psychographic combinations of our clients' target markets, we narrow down the ideal customer to the most specific individual that we can find, and scale based on that data. I want my customers to be able to invest $1 in my marketing and $3, $5 $10 or even $20 back. Hyper-targeting allows me to do that, and I take pride in what I do because I know that I'm helping to connect customers in need with the brands that can help them. But I digress, let's summarize!

When building a community around a brand on Social Media, the first step is to identify the ideal community by defining both the purpose of the community and the population to whom the community is built for. Understanding the purpose, more specifically what problem or interest is the focal point around which people will gather, and the population, or people who exhibit certain demographic and psychographic qualities most similar to that of the ideal customer, of a community is fundamental to building a targeted community around a brand on Social Media.

Grow The Community

The second step in building a community around a brand on Social Media is to grow the community. Due to the nature of Social Media, "growth" of a community is extremely difficult to measure. For the sake of this paper, however, growth will be measured in two ways in an effort to gage both long and short-term growth. First is the number of people directly attributed to a brand's Social Media platforms, for example likes on a Facebook business page or followers on an Instagram account. This type of growth is long-term and quantitatively effective, but fickle as an independent measurement of growth. While an individual might like or follow a brand on Social Media, that does not mean that individual is an active part of the community, nor is it evident that they see all of the information shared by the brand. However, there is no other method to date which more effectively measures how large a brand's Social Media community is than the total number of likes and followers on its platforms.

Second is the amount of engagement by people with a brand on those platforms. This type of growth is short-term, as it applies on a daily basis in the form of likes, comments, shares, etc. on individual posts. For example, a Facebook post with 700 comments and 1,400 likes clearly has more engagement than a separate post with 4 likes and a single comment. Like the first, engagement is quantitatively effective but not as meaningful as an independent measurement tool. Only together are these tools useful metrics for growth. Together, the long-term growth measurement gives an estimate of how many people could be a part of the community as a whole while the short-term numbers show how many people are actively participating. Regardless of how a brand decides to measure growth, it needs to fundamentally understand how to achieve it. To be sure, there is not a panacea to growth. However, I want to discuss two fundamental elements of a growth strategy that are crucial to any growth strategy for developing a community around a brand on Social Media: targeting and positioning.

Targeting is crucial for community growth, and can be broken down into two main questions: who and where. Since we discussed the "who" question earlier in this paper, I want to focus on where to find sources for community growth, starting with the current customer base. When a sale is made, that consumer is an incredible potential resource. According to Action Coach, "if a business makes a concerted effort to identify loyal customers and then offer them such a high level of service that they become cheerleaders for the business, the investment pays off many times over by expanding the customer base with premium customers acquired via raving fans." A brand that makes a habit of converting every single customer into a loyal, raving one will find that the current customer base is an incredibly effective and convenient foundation for its community on Social Media. Practically, this isn't a difficult process if the service or product is of superior quality; a brand must simply offer something of value in return for participation in its community. For example, a subscription based app brand could offer a free trial to those who like the brand's Facebook page or follow its Instagram account.

The next sources come from other brands that serve similar market segments, but in two capacities. The first is your competition. If two brands are in direct competition, then by definition they will be targeting the same people. Especially for new brands, paying attention to where the competition is deploying their marketing efforts can yield dividends for both the brand and the consumer. Not only does the competition face a potential loss of market share, but the consumer also has more options to choose from! For example,

Facebook has a feature called "Groups," where people can congregate via ongoing discussion. A lawn-care business owner who needs more customers might join a group specifically for local botanists and occasionally plug his business' brand. Not only is there nothing stopping similar business owners from doing the exact same thing and taking market share, but the botanists would probably appreciate other options to drive down the going rate for lawn care. The next source comes from other brands that target the same people but are not your competition. For example, the lawn-care business owner might reach out to the owner of a local garden supply shop. While these businesses target a very similar market segment, they are not in competition and could potentially benefit from a partnership. Practically, the lawn-care service could recommend the garden supply shop on a Facebook, and vice versa. By doing this, both brands can benefit by reaching the other's community.

The next places to target are your industry or subject matter hubs, but in two main categories: Social Media platforms and other online hubs. Other online hubs, in this paper, will refer to blogs, forums, or websites that aren't Social Media platforms. While the line separating these two categories is fuzzy at best, there is a distinction:

blogs, forums or websites that aren't Social Media platforms are places to *create* content online, whereas Social Media platforms are places to *share* content online. For any specific industry, the diversity and scope of Social Media platforms are endless. Therefore, it is more useful to pick a few, specific platforms to target than to try to hit them all. For example, a law firm might find potential community members on Avvo, a Social Media platform that functions as an online legal services marketplace. On Avvo, there are two separate functions for lawyers and everyone else. While anyone can log on and ask a question, an attorney has the option to answer those questions. There is a natural connection made during the transfer of knowledge, and it is a great place for a lawyer to add to his or her community from. Once the lawyer answers the question, he or she could simply message the individual who posted the question and invite that individual to like the law firm's Facebook page and join the community.

Like Social Media platforms, there are tons of other online hubs for every industry, so it is more effective to focus on a few. The biggest online hubs that I want to analyze are blogs and forums, as they are not only extremely popular, but are also great places to target community members. A blog, according to Susan Gunelius, 20-year marketing veteran and President & CEO of KeySplash Creative, Inc., is "a website consisting of entries (also called posts) appearing in reverse chronological order with the most recent entry appearing first (similar in format to a daily journal)." Blogs are a fantastic place to find relevant community members because each blog post, and usually the entire blog, has a specific subject and audience already. For example, Social Media Examiner is a popular blog on Social Media. Each blog post gets shared and read across a plethora of Social Media platforms, meaning an immense number of people see each post and view Social Media Examiner as an expert. People want to do business with experts. If you can't put together a fully functional blog, then a great way to target potential community members is to leave comments or reply to comments on other peoples' blogs. Blogs typically become more popular over time, so it is up to the individual representing the brand to decide whether to invest time in a smaller, more intimate blog or a larger, more visible blog. Forums are similar to blogs in the capacity that it is an ongoing discussion about a certain topic but different because all users add to the discussion as opposed to one-person blogging. Like blogs, forums are great for finding relevant community members because each post has a specific subject and the forum as a whole has a specific audience. For example, a computer mouse brand would probably find a video game forum a spectacular place to target potential members of its community. Regardless of how you choose to target your audience, it is important to make sure you do so precisely.

Brand positioning is the second fundamental element of growing a community. Brand positioning is defined as "the process of positioning your brand in the mind of your customers" (Bueno and Jeffrey 2014), so it is crucial that a brand positions itself correctly. While there are an infinite number of ways to position a brand, I want to analyze one method in particular: positioning the brand as an expert in the industry. The value of being recognized as an expert is substantial. "People trust experts. People believe in experts. Most of all, people choose to do business with experts" (Pienaar). For growth purposes, people tend to follow and listen to experts. Instead of having to go out and find community members, they will naturally be attracted to the brand as an authoritative source in the industry. Experts are thought-leaders and earn the trust of their customers and peers through expertise, experience and the ability to continuously solve problems that affect their industry. While being recognized as an expert has a plethora advantages for business, it is difficult for a brand to be positioned as an expert. For obvious reasons, people associate other people as experts, so "the best way to position yourself [and your brand] as an expert is to have an opinion and use your voice to define your brand" (Pienaar). The distinction here is subtle but important, people are experts and people define brands. Therefore, in order to position a brand as an expert, all of the people who represent the brand in the public eye have to be seen as experts since they collectively define the brand over time. While this is an extremely difficult, perpetual process, the rewards are limitless. When a brand recognized as an expert in an industry is a foundation of knowledge for people who are coming together for a cause on Social Media, the brand will have a significantly higher chance of thriving, growing and becoming a permanent entity.

Manage The Community

The third and final step for building a targeted community around a brand on Social Media is managing the community. There are various styles for managing a community, and each brand must fine-tune their own strategy for their own community. However, I want to discuss two fundamental elements. The first is creating or curating valuable content for the members of the community. One characteristic of Social Media is that it is an ongoing discussion; without that aspect, people lose interest and stop coming back. In order to keep the community alive, a brand needs to consistently create fresh content to keep people coming back. That being said, it can't just be any poorly written article – the content has to be high quality! Because there is an immense amount of new content created everyday, the content that is shared on behalf of the brand has to cut through the clutter. To put it in perspective, about "2.7 million blog posts are published every day" (Stevens 2016), and those are being added to the already immense amount of content already in existence. For a brand, this means having somebody, or a team of people, constantly finding or creating high quality, engaging and relevant content. While this is a daunting task, the rewards are well worth the work. According to a recent article by Neil Patel, co-founder of Crazy Egg, Hello Bar and KISSmetrics, not only do "78% of consumers believe that organizations providing custom content are interested in building good relationships," but "61% of consumers' buying decision is influenced by custom content!" By creating and providing valuable content, the community will want to keep coming back, and chances are they will share some of it with their network. In addition, a brand can develop its reputation as an expert by consistently sharing and creating content that adds value to the lives of its community. The demand for an immense amount of content also allows a brand to subtly promote its own products or services. Instead of blasting out infomercials on its products, successful brands seamlessly weave self-promotion into the over-arching content creation strategy. For example, a fishing gear brand could provide its community with Wildlife and Fisheries reports, articles from prominent ichthyologists (fish experts), and tutorials on how to use different fishing equipment. All of these pieces of content would appeal to expert fishermen, so the brand is building a reputation as a hub for all sorts of fishermen, wildlife enthusiasts, etc. Naturally, some of the tutorials on fishing equipment would be the brand's products, and that type of content would be perfect for that community. However the brand chooses to develop content, the needs of the people should be in mind the entire time.

The second aspect of community management is the single most important factor in building a targeted community on Social Media: developing relationships with and between the members of the community. While great content will make an individual come back to a brand's Social Media page, meaningful relationships with real people in and behind the brand's community will make an individual a permanent part of that community. As Dr. Peck said, "the seeds of community reside in humanity," and a community on Social Media is no different. Without real relationships, without genuine human interaction, there is no community. There are an infinite ways to build a relationship, but each brand's community will be different. Those who are managing the community are responsible for engaging every single member of the community. In the early stages of community development, it is a lot easier to get to know each individual member, and the relationships will be more personal (and therefore more meaningful). One effective method is to ask the community members questions. By asking for an opinion, a community manager can start a discussion and show that the voice of each individual community member holds weight. If, and hopefully when, the community starts to respond, it is crucial to keep the momentum going by any means necessary. As the community grows, it can be a struggle to figure out the best way to keep everyone happy, but the community manager must test the waters. Share different types of content, bring in guest bloggers, ask the people what they want, anything! For a while, it will be a struggle to keep the community growing and managed at the same time. Once the community reaches a certain critical mass, however, it will become a self-sustaining, ongoing discussion where people are making relationships with each other independent of the community manager. Until that time, however, it is crucial for the community manager to constantly try and build relationships with and among the community members. Remember, people are people. The same things that make individuals like someone offline are typically what can also make them like a brand online. Care for the community; nurture it like a newly planted seed, and one day it can grow into a tree that lasts for hundreds of years.

Conclusion

Building a targeted community on Social Media is a three-step process: identification, growth and management. More specifically, these fundamentals include understanding who the ideal population is by defining the purpose of the community and the demographics and psychographics of the ideal consumer, fostering growth based on effective targeting and brand positioning tactics, and providing sufficient community management through content creation and relationship development. By using the three-step process, a brand is providing the perfect environment for relationship and eventually community development. As Phil Brown said, community is built from five core elements: a sense of place, common interests and perspectives, a sense of coherence and identity, meaningful relationships and diversity. Social Media provides the place. The demographic and psychographic research provides grounds for common interests and perspectives. The purpose of the community provides a sense of coherence and identity. Targeting will attract sub-communities from various places. Quality content can consistently promote discussion and experts can engage and unite the people with meaningful relationships. This three-step process provides the fundamentals to understand and successfully execute development of a community around a brand on Social Media.

Bibliography

Andreas M. Kaplan, Michael Haenlein, Users of the world, unite! The challenges and opportunities of Social Media, Business Horizons, Volume 53, Issue 1, January–February 2010, Pages 59-68, ISSN 0007-6813, http://dx.doi.org/10.1016/j.bushor.2009.09.003. (http://www.sciencedirect.com/science/article/pii/S0007681309001232)

Brown, Phil. "Who Is the Community?" (n.d.): n. pag. *Who Is the Community?* Brown University. Web. 19 Apr. 2016. <https://www.brown.edu/research/research-ethics/sites/brown.edu.research.research-ethics/files/uploads/Who%20is%20the%20community%20-%20Phil%20Brown_0.pdf>.

Bueno, BJ, and Scott Jeffrey. "How to Create Strong Positioning in Your Market." *The Cult Branding Company.* The Cult Branding Company, 6 May 2014. Web. <http://cultbranding.com/ceo/create-strong-brand-positioning-strategy/>.

Duggan, Maeve. "The Demographics of Social Media Users." *Pew Research Center Internet Science Tech RSS.* Pew Research Center, 19 Aug. 2015. Web. 01 May 2016. <http://www.pewinternet.org/2015/08/19/the-demographics-of-social-media-users/>.

"11 Ways to Double Your Customer Base in Four Weeks." *Whitepaper - Franchise Rep* (n.d.): n. pag. *Action Coach.* Action Coach. Web. 1 May 2016. <http://www.actioncoach.com/_downloads/whitepaper-FranchiseRep4.pdf>.

Gunelius, Susan. "What Is a Blog?" *Blogging*. About.com, Dec. 2014. Web. 01 May 2016. <http://weblogs.about.com/od/startingablog/p/WhatIsABlog.htm>.

"Hear the World's Sounds." *SoundCloud*. N.p., n.d. Web. 01 May 2016. <https://soundcloud.com/>.

"How to Build an Engaged Social Audience." *Wyzowl*. Wyzowl, n.d. Web. 23 Mar. 2016. <https://drive.google.com/file/d/0B4j3dp2ZJqzeSDBfZnVTQnZSN Uk/view?usp=sharing>.

Howden, Lindsay, and Julie Meyer. "Age and Sex Composition: 2010." *2010 Census Briefs* (2011): n. pag. *Census.gov*. United States Census Bureau, May 2011. Web. <http://www.census.gov/prod/cen2010/briefs/c2010br-03.pdf>.

"Let's Explore the Value of Custom Content." *Ext Marketing Inc.* Ext Marketing, 27 Apr. 2016. Web. 02 May 2016. <http://ext-marketing.com/marketing-articles/lets-explore-value-custom-content/>.

Marcyes, Lisa. "How Brands Can Create Lasting Relationships on Social Media." *Marketo Marketing Blog Best Practices and Thought Leadership*. Marketo, 18 Apr. 2016. Web. 02 May 2016. <http://blog.marketo.com/2016/04/how-brands-can-create-lasting-relationships-on-social-media.html>.

Meng, Andy. "What Is Pinterest, and How Does It Work?" *Search Engine Optimization*. Infront Webworks, 20 Jan. 2014. Web. <http://www.infront.com/blogs/the-infront-blog/2014/1/20/what-is-pinterest-and-how-does-it-work#>.

"Number of Worldwide Social Network Users 2010-2018." *Statista*. Statista, n.d. Web. 23 Mar. 2016. <http://www.statista.com/statistics/278414/number-of-worldwide-social-network-users/>.

Patel, Neil. "38 Content Marketing Stats That Every Marketer Needs to Know." *Neil Patel 38 Content Marketing Stats That Every Marketer Needs to Know Comments*. Neil Patel, 21 Jan. 2016. Web. 02 May 2016. <http://neilpatel.com/2016/01/21/38-content-marketing-stats-that-every-marketer-needs-to-know/>.

Peck, M. Scott, M.d. "The True Meaning of Community." *The Different Drum: Community Making and Peace by M. Scott Peck, M.D. CHAPTER III The True Meaning of Community* (n.d.): n. pag. *Www.entcom.eu*. Entcom. Web. 19 Apr. 2016. <http://www.entcom.eu/wp-content/uploads/2015/10/Entcom-WS-Report-Annex2.pdf>.

Pienaar, Adii. "Branding Yourself As An Expert In..." *Clarity RSS*. Clarity, n.d. Web. 02 May 2016. <http://blog.clarity.fm/branding-yourself-as-an-expert-in/>.

Porta, Mandy. "How to Define Your Target Market." *Inc.com*. Inc, 04 Dec. 2016. Web. 19 Apr. 2016. <http://www.inc.com/guides/2010/06/defining-your-target-market.html>.

Smith, Craig. "80 Amazing Snapchat Statistics." *Expanded Ramblings*. DMR, 02 Feb. 2014. Web. 04 May 2016. <http://expandedramblings.com/index.php/snapchat-statistics/>.

Smith, Craig. "By the Numbers: 270 Amazing Pinterest Statistics." *Digital Stat Articles*. Expanded Ramblings, 13 Apr. 2016. Web. <http://expandedramblings.com/index.php/pinterest-stats/>.

Stevens, John. "Internet Stats & Facts for 2016." *Hosting Facts.* Hosting Facts Ltd., 21 Apr. 2016. Web. 02 May 2016. <https://hostingfacts.com/internet-facts-stats-2016/>.

Sugars, Brad. "The Fastest Way to Find New Customers." *Entrepreneur.* Entrepreneur, 23 Oct. 2007. Web. 01 May 2016. <https://www.entrepreneur.com/article/185880>.

"Super Bowl: Retail Sales Growth by Category, 2015 | Statistic." *Statista: The Statistics Portal.* Statista, n.d. Web. 01 May 2016. <http://www.statista.com/statistics/508292/super-bowl-retail-dollar-sales-growth-united-states-category/>.

Upfront Analytics Team. "Understanding the Importance of Demographics in Marketing." *Blog.* Upfront Analytics, 27 May 2015. Web. 25 Apr. 2016. <http://upfrontanalytics.com/understanding-the-importance-of-demographics-in-marketing/>.

Zemmels, David R., PhD. "Youth And New Media: Constructing Meaning And Identity In Networked Spaces." Diss. U of Utah, 2011. University of Utah. Web. 23 Mar. 2016. <http://content.lib.utah.edu/utils/getfile/collection/etd3/id/347/filename/434.pdf>.

www.ingramcontent.com/pod-product-compliance
Lightning Source LLC
Chambersburg PA
CBHW070749210326
41520CB00016B/4647